After the Ark

Lord Jesus — as we go through life on
in the world you created — helps us
always to treat with respect those
creatures of this planet — from the humblest
insect to the most magnificent animals
of the jungle.

May we never harm, by neglect,
carelessness or indifference, the pets
that we have taken into our our home

ELIZABETH JENNINGS

After the Ark

OXFORD UNIVERSITY PRESS

OXFORD LONDON NEW YORK

Oxford University Press, Walton Street, Oxford OX2 6DP

OXFORD LONDON GLASGOW
NEW YORK TORONTO MELBOURNE WELLINGTON
IBADAN NAIROBI DAR ES SALAAM CAPE TOWN
KUALA LUMPUR SINGAPORE JAKARTA HONG KONG TOKYO
DELHI BOMBAY CALCUTTA MADRAS KARACHI

British Library Cataloguing in Publication Data

Jennings, Elizabeth
    After the ark.
    I. Title
    821'.9'14   PR6060.E52A/   77–30613
    ISBN 0–19–276044–0

*Printed in Great Britain by
The Bowering Press Ltd,
Plymouth*

Contents

The Animals' Chorus

Once there was nothing but water and air. The air
Broke into constellations, waters withdrew.
The sun was born and itself hatched out first light.
Rocks appeared and sand, and on the rocks
There was movement. Under the sea
Something tender survived, not yet a fish,
A nameless object floating. This was how we

Began and how you later followed us,
Much, much later, long before clocks or sun-dials,
Long before time was discovered.
The sun stared hard and the moon looked back and mountains
Pierced the air. Snow was formed, this earth
Was gently beginning to live.

We were your fore-runners, we with fins and tails,
With wings and legs. Under the sun we crawled
To life. How good the air was, how sweet the green
Leaves, the rock-pools, the sturdy trees. And flowers

Flaunted such fragrance we wandered among them, clung
To their petals or, out of the blue and widespread air,
Descended, drew in our wings and settled where
You now stand or sit or walk. We know
So much about you. We are your family tree
But you have power over us for you can name,
And naming is like possession. It's up to you
To give us our liberty or to make us tame.

The Fish's Warning

Stay by the water, stand on your shadow, stare
At my quick gliding, my darting body. You're made of air
And I of water. I do not know if you mean to throw
Your line, I move very fast, swim with fins much quicker
Than your thin arms. Rushes will hide me and will
Darken me. I'm a pulse of silver, something the moon
   tossed down.
I am frail for your finding but one whom only the night
   can drown.

The Ladybird's Story

It was a roadway to me.
So many meeting-places and directions.
It was smooth, polished, sometimes it shook a little
But I did not tumble off.
I heard you say, and it was like a siren,
"A ladybird. Good luck. Perhaps some money."
I did not understand.
Suddenly I was frightened, fearful of falling
Because you lifted your hand.

And then I saw your eyes,
Glassy moons always changing shape,
Sometimes suns in eclipse.
I watched the beak, the peak of your huge nose
And the island of your lips.
I was afraid but you were not. I have
No sting. I do not wound.
I carry a brittle coat. It does not protect.
I thought you would blow me away but superstition
Saved me. You held your hand now in one position,
Gentled me over the veins and arteries.
But it was not I you cared about but money.
You see I have watched you with flies.

The Cabbage White Butterfly

I look like a flower you could pick. My delicate wings
Flutter over the cabbages. I don't make
Any noise ever. I'm among silent things.
    Also I easily break.

I have seen the nets in your hands. At first I thought
A cloud had come down but then I noticed you
With your large pink hand and arm. I was nearly caught
    But fortunately I flew

Away in time, hid while you searched, then took
To the sky, was out of your reach. Like a nameless flower
I tried to appear. Can't you be happy to look?
    Must you possess with your power?

The Moth's Plea

I am a disappointment
And much worse.
You hear a flutter, you expect a brilliance of wings,
Colours dancing, a bright
Flutter, but then you see
A brown, bedraggled creature
With a shamefaced, unclean look
Darting upon your curtains and clothes,
Fighting against the light.
I hate myself. It's no wonder you hate me.

I meddle among your things,
I make a meal out of almost any cloth,
I hide in cupboards and scare
Any who catch me unaware.
I am your enemy—the moth.

You try to keep me away
But I'm wily and when I do
Manage to hide, you chase me, beat me, put
Horrible-smelling balls to poison me.
Have you ever thought what it's like to be
A parasite,
Someone who gives you a fright,
Who envies the rainbow colours of the bright
Butterflies who hover round flowers all day?

O please believe that I do understand how it feels
To be awake in and be afraid of the night.

The Spider's Confession

You with your looms and wheels and every kind of machine,
Don't you marvel at the intricate lace I spin?
Many of you are skilful but have you seen
Working under your hands such delicacy, such thin,
Easily breakable patterns? You think it strange

That one with a squashy, dark and ugly body,
Can make such a wonder. I wish that I could convince
All of you that it hurts to carry around
A creature so greatly at odds with the work it spins.
Some of you are revolted at sight of me
And quickly wash me down drains. All that I ask is that you
At least allow me to do
My work. That is all I honestly want you to see.

Wasp in a Room

Chase me, follow me round the room, knock over
Chairs and tables, bruise knees, spill books. High
I am then. If you climb up to me I go
Down. I have ways of detecting your least
Movements. I have radar you did not
Invent. You are afraid of me. I can
Sting hard. Ah but watch me bask in
The, to you, unbearable sun. I sport with it, am
Its jester and also its herald. Fetch a
Fly whisk. I scorn such. You must invent stings
For yourselves or else leave me alone, small, flying,
Buzzing tiger who have made a jungle out of the room
   you thought safe,
Secure from all hurts and prying.

The Snake's Warning

A coil of power,
A twist of speed,
Hider in grass,
Content in jungles,
Footless, wingless,
I have powers beasts lack,
Strength birds seek
In clean skies which
Are not my home.
If footsteps approach
Or I hear a twig
Break I alert
At once. My tongue
Means painful death.
Keep your hands off me.

There are men, a few,
With a special gift
To whom I surrender.
I sway to the sound
Of their flutes but I keep
My glance upon them.
They hypnotize me,
Don't ask me how
Or when or why,
If *you* want to be safe,
Keep away, don't try
To tame me with flutes.
If you do, you will die.

The Earthworm's Monologue

Birds prey on me, fish are fond of my flesh.
My body is like a sausage, it lacks the snake's
Sinuous splendour and colour. Yes, I'm absurd.
Yet I also till and soften the soil, I prepare
The way for flowers, Spring depends upon me
At least a little. Mock me if you will,
Cut me in half, I'll come together again.
But haven't you felt a fool, hated your shape,
Wanted to hide? If so I am your friend;
I would sympathise with you were I not so busy
But bend down over me, you who are not yet tall
And be proud of all you contain in a body so small.

The Frogs' History

You caught and carried us, pleased with yourselves.
We were only blobs of black in jars.

You knew what we'd become, were glad to wait.
How hectically we swam in that glass cage!

And there was never hope of an escape.
You put us on a shelf with more care than

You generally move. We were a hope,
A something-to-look-forward to, a change,

Almost a conjuring trick. Some sleight of nature
Would, given time, change us to your possessions.

We would be green and glossy, wet to touch.
"Take them away," squeamish grown-ups would

Call out. Not you. You longed to hold us in
Your dry palms with surprising gentleness

And with a sense of unexpected justice
Would let us go, wanted to see us leap

And watch our eyes which never seem to sleep,
Hear our hideous but lively croak.

We know as well as you we are a joke.

The Bats' Plea

Ignore the stories which say
We shall fly to and tangle your hair,
That you are wise if you dread
Our mouse-like bodies, the way
Our wings fan out and spread
In gloom, in dusty air.

Eagles are lucky to be
Thought of in terms of light
And glory. Half-bird, half-beast,
We're an anomaly.
But, clinging to darkness we rest
And, like stars, belong to the night.

The Swallows' Speech

We are the bearers of sun, we take
Its rays with us, it rides our wings
And trusts its gold to us. The sky
Enlarges southward, opens for
Our passage. Watch our nestlings fly
After. We carry all warm things.

You in the Winter only know
Our arrow ways in dreams. We keep
A little glow within your minds,
We stoke your loving and your sleep.
Listen, our wings are coming back.
Summer is on. We tell you so.

Gull Thought

Shall I descend? Shall I allow
A buffet of wind to take me? Shall
I hover to stillness over the tides,
Smelling the salt, waiting to pounce
And bruise the waves? The sun's gold slides
Over my wings. I am wide awake
And the earth is mine to take.

I descend to a place of waves and hands,
To water-filled air, to spume and to
five fingers holding me food. I am
August and insolent. Hands, wait there!
I will skim the horizon before I turn,
A tide of my own, and grasp the bread,
Following instinct, possessing the air.

The Rooks' Chorus

Our homes are high,
We sway in the sun and wind
And are not afraid
Of a stormy sky.
At night we sleep
Close to the moon and stars.
Think of us as the deep
Note of the songs which fill your mind
As a lullaby.

Early risers are we.
We want to veer
About as the sun rises
Magnificently.
We open our wings
To protect more fragile things.
Look up at us when you wake
And the turns and curves we make
And fashion your day with the songs
We sing to ease you awake.

The Robin's Song

I am cheerful. You can
Depend on me. I'm around
All the year. In the rain,
When frost is on the ground
Or the sun is dancing, I'm here,
Bright in colour and sound.

Other birds are less stout,
Sing flawless songs in Spring,
Look more beautiful, there's no doubt.
I am always pleased when you fling
Crumbs to me. Yes, I am happy.
Isn't that everything?

The Sparrows' Chorus

How often you forget about us! We are
About all through the year.
Our feathers are drab, beside other birds we appear
Nonentities, no fashion parades for us.
Nobody makes a fuss
Of us and really we don't care,
At least, not too much.
But we are faithful, whatever the weather we stay
Among you. And don't think we're ungrateful for the food
Some of you like to toss.
We need it badly. We can lose half our weight
On an icy night. We depend a lot on you.

Often, we have to admit, we wish we wore
Flamboyant colours. A yellow, a red, a blue.
The robin is lucky and all the tits are too.
But perhaps our smallness is noticeable. Beside
A starling or blackbird we are almost invisible
But don't forget we are here,
Domestic creatures, never flying far.
Just to exist through an English climate is
Remarkable.
It's almost a miracle simply that we are.

The Thrush Confides

The truth about me is I am
One who enjoys life, who feels
Happy most of the time.
Whatever weather may come—
Wind, rain, enormous falls
Of snow—I feel at home
And would like you to feel much the same.

And please don't imagine that I
Am stupid or priggish. I'm not.
I know I'm not handsome, not one
Who people point at and cry
"What a very remarkable sight."
I like being left alone
To find worms, look about, feel the sun.

The Owl's Request

Do not be frightened of me.
I am a night-time creature. When the earth is still,
When trees are shadows of shadows,
When only the moon and its attendant stars
Enlarge the night, when the smallest sound is shrill
And may wake you up and frighten you,
I am about with my friendly "Tu-whit, tu whoo".

My face is kindly but also mysterious.
People call me wise.
Perhaps they do so because I sometimes close my eyes
And seem to be thinking.
The way I think is not like yours. I need
No thick philosopher's book;
I can tell the truth of the world with a look
But I do not speak about
What I see there. Think of me then
As the certainty in your wandering nights.
I can soothe men
And will snatch you out of your doubt,
Bear you away to the stars and moon
And to sleep and dawn. So lie
And listen to my lullaby.

The Cuckoo's Speech

What a very bad example I set
But never mind.
I have the best of all worlds. I get
Applause and kind
Words from all when they hear the sound
Of me. Winter's behind

And I prove Spring's arrived. Forget the way
I use the homes
Of others, set up house there, always lay
My eggs in the warm
Hard-worked-for nests. O yes, you can certainly say
To me all good luck comes.

The Cockerel Proclaims

I am proud of my pride.
I open the doors of morning.
I shout the trees awake,
Circle your towns with a high,
Magnificent, self-controlled cry.

One by one I snuff out the stars
And I am the first colours,
A reminder of the rainbow,
A singer shaming your small
Complaining voices. I'm tall

And proud of my flaring height.
I am the sun's true herald.
I wind up the small birds' voices,
And tell you it's worth getting up
As I lock the doors of the night.

The Fieldmouse's Monologue

Didn't you know how frightened I was when I came
For shelter in your room? I am not tame.
You looked enormous when I saw you first.
I rushed to the hole I had made, took refuge there,
Crouched behind paper you thrust at me, shivered with fear.
I had smelt some chocolate. The kitchen was warm below
And outside there was frost and, one whole night, great snow.

I only guessed you were frightened too when you
Called out loudly, deafeningly to me.
My ears are small but my hearing strong, you see.
You pushed old papers against my hole and so
I had to climb into a drawer. You did not know
That I could run so high. I felt your hand,
Like my world in shadow, shudder across me and
I scuttled away but felt a kind of bond
With you in your huge fear.
Was I the only friend near?

The Hedgehog's Explanation

I move very slowly,
I would like to be friendly,
Yet my prickly back has a look of danger. You might
Suppose I were ready for war or at least a fight
With a cat on the wall, a gather of birds, but no,
My prickles damage nobody, so you

Must be gentle with me, you with your huge shadow,
Your footsteps like claps of thunder,
The terrible touch of your hands.
Listen to me : I am a ball of fear,
Terror is what I know best,
What I live with and dream about.
Put out a saucer of milk for me,
Keep me from roads and cars.
If *you* want to look after someone,
Take care of me
And give me at least the pretence I am safe and free.

The Rabbit's Advice

I have been away too long.
Some of you think I am only a nursery tale,
One which you've grown out of.
Or perhaps you saw a movie and laughed at my ears
But rather envied my carrot.
I must tell you that I exist.

I'm a puff of wool leaping across a field,
Quick to all noises,
Smelling my burrow of safety.
I am easily frightened. A bird
Is tame compared to me.
Perhaps you have seen my fat white cousin who sits,
Constantly twitching his nose,
Behind bars in a hutch at the end of a garden.
If not, imagine those nights when you lie awake
Afraid to turn over, afraid
Of night and dawn and sleep.
Terror is what I am made
Of partly, partly of speed.

But I am a figure of fun.
I have no dignity
Which means I am never free.
So, when you are frightened or being teased, think of
My twitching whiskers, my absurd white puff of a tail,
Of all that I mean by "me"
And my ludicrous craving for love.

The Sheep's Confession

I look stupid, much like a dirty heap of snow
The Winter left.
I have nothing to draw your attention, nothing for show,
Except the craft

Which shears me and leaves me looking even more
Unintelligent.
I do not wonder you laugh when you see my bare
Flesh like a tent

Whose guy-ropes broke. But listen, I have one thing
To charm and delight—
The lamb I drop when Winter is turning to Spring.
His coat is white,

Purer than mine and he wears socks of black wool.
He can move
And prance. I am proud of a son so beautiful
And so worthy of love.

The Deers' Request

We are the disappearers.
You may never see us, never,
But if you make your way through a forest
Stepping lightly and gently,
Not plucking or touching or hurting,
You may one day see a shadow
And after the shadow a patch
Of speckled fawn, a glint
Of a horn.
    Those signs mean us.

O chase us never. Don't hurt us.
We who are male carry antlers
Horny, tough, like trees,
But we are terrified creatures,
Are quick to move, are nervous
Of the flutter of birds, of the quietest
Footfall, are frightened of every noise.

If you would learn to be gentle,
To be quiet and happy alone,
Think of our lives in deep forests,
Of those who hunt us and haunt us
And drive us into the ocean.
If you love to play by yourself
Content in that liberty,
Think of us being hunted,
Tell those men to let us be.

The Riding School

We are at grass now and the emerald meadow
Highlights our polished coats. All afternoon
You trotted, cantered us. How mild we were,
Our bodies were at one
With yours. Now we are cropping at the shadow
We throw. We scarcely stir.

You never saw us wild or being broken
In. We tossed our saddles off and ran
With streaming manes. Like Pegasus almost
We scorned the air. A man
Took long to tame us. Let your words be spoken
Gently. You own the freedom we have lost.

The Black Cat's Conversation

Do not suppose
Because I keep to the fire,
Am out half the night,
Sleep where I fall,
Eye you with stares
Like your finest marbles,
That I am not conscious
Of your slightest changes
In mood. I never
Miss your temper
Although you attempt
To disguise it. I know

How envious you are
Of my lithe body,
My lack of self-consciousness,
My glossy coat,
My imperious air.
All this is instinct,
Something you've lost
Except when you cower
From the rats I bring in,
Proud of my haul.
I am proud of my pride
And I always win.

The Lion Cub

My fur is soft. I am not a lion yet.
You can tease me a little, treat me like a pet.

The keeper is feeding my parents. Trust me to
Be playful. I can warm and comfort you.

Forget the forests and jungle, the great sun-face
Of my father. He has violence and grace

And I have neither yet. For a little time
I am a prince locked safe in a nursery rhyme.

Finale For The Animals

Some with cruelty came, sharp-fanged and clawed,
Tore at the air searching for food which, found,
They ate in an instant—new leaves, the tall and small
Flowers. Carnivores were
Worse, hunters of blood, smellers of victims
More miles away than our instruments measure or we
Imagine. Meanwhile the jungle listened and looked.
The parrot kept its beak shut, the slithering snake
Stilled to a coil. The stars were listening, the sun's
Burning paused at the tear and rampage of
A striped or spotted creature. This was the time
Before we were.

Now we have caged and enclosed but not enchanted
Most of these. Now full of power we are not
Gentle with flowers, pull too hard, break the admired
Rose with abandonment. We should know better.

You have heard of the ark and Noah. Most likely it
Was a local event or a myth but remember men
Bow down to the myths they create.
Perhaps we were kindest, most gentle,
Most at our best
When we coupled all creatures and launched them forth
    in an ark.
Imagination was gracious then indeed,
Gracious too when we thought up the speeding dove,
Feathery emblem of peace whiter than clouds, its wings
Combing and calming the breakers. The waters stilled.

You have heard now of some of these, learnt of their habits.
Do not haunt zoos too often, do not demand
Affection too often from rabbits or cats or dogs,
Do not tame if taming hurts.
Be grateful for such variety of manners,
For the diverse universe.
Above all respect the smallest of all these creatures
As you are awed by the stars.